SUMMARY OF

THE

ROOM WHERE

IT HAPPENED

A WHITE HOUSE MEMOIR

BY JOHN BOLTON

Proudly Brought To You By
Oliver Graham

ISBN: 978-1-952639-23-4

Table of Contents

EXECUTIVE SUMMARY

Quite a number of books have filled the shelves ever since Donald Trump assumed office as the President of the United States. *The Room Where It Happened* goes beyond many of these to provide an all-inclusive, extensive account of the Trump Administration. This book was written by a top official who had unrestricted access to the President. If you ever had a burning desire to truly know what happens in the Oval Office, who Trump truly is, and a host of others that characterize the White House and the man behind the desk, then this is for you.

CHAPTER 1: THE LONG MARCH TO A WEST WING CORNER OFFICE

KEY TAKEAWAYS
- As National Security Advisor, there is a huge, unending pile of challenges you get to meet with.
- No explanation would be enough to adequately capture the transformation that took place within the Trump Administration.
- Having been poorly served by the previous set of people in government, Trump became highly suspicious of people.

There is one incredibly attractive feature that comes with being the National Security Advisor. This is it: there is a vast, unending pile of challenges you get to meet with. In all honesty, if you're not cut out for anything resembling stress, risk, chaos, and indecision while being loaded with tons of information, decisions to make, and a vast amount of work, I will advise that you take another offer. The job is demanding; it is outrightly exhausting. Unfortunately, persons on the outside find this difficult to comprehend. As a matter of fact, I find it challenging to explain to outsiders how difficult a task is to fix the different parts together, which in many cases, hardly gets fixed in lucid terms.

I cannot provide an explanation that captures the transformation that took place within the Trump Administration. I mean, even if I did try, no explanation would be enough to describe it adequately. There is a general tale that Washington holds about Trump's trajectory. Personally, I believe that this version of the truth appeals only to intellectually lazy individuals. This theory posits that Trump had always been unconventional. He had just found himself in an entirely new world, and for the first fifteen months of his administration, his actions and decisions were checked and controlled by some key players in government. As a result of all these factors, he was hesitant to act. However, as the days rolled by, he became more confident of himself, the government officials who served as checks on him left, things took a downturn, and Trump became surrounded by men that were ready to do his bidding, agreeing with him on all matters.

There are some authentic parts of this story. However, the general picture tells a straightforward tale. The key players in government created problems that lingered, not as a result of successfully managing Trump, but from doing the exact opposite. They failed to establish order but succeeded in doing things that showed how much they were about their personal interests, publicly trivializing several distinct goals that Trump had. All their actions culminated in feeding Trump's mindset, which was already suspicious at the time. As a result, it became rather difficult for those who came to have genuine, sincere relations with the President.

For a long time, I felt that the National Security Advisor had a major role in ensuring that the President had a concrete understanding of the options before him when faced with making decisions. I also believed that it was the duty of the National Security Advisor to ensure that the appropriate establishments executed the decisions. Of course, the National Security Council process was going to differ from President to President. However, these were fundamental objectives that the entire process ought to achieve.

Sadly, however, having been poorly served by the previous set of people in government, Trump became highly suspicious of people, second-guessing their every motive, uncovering conspiracies, and worse still, remaining utterly clueless on how to run the White House, talk more of the Federal government. There is something to note, however. The key players in government are not entirely responsible for this mindset, which Trump had. Truth is, Trump is Trump, and this isn't even a debate. I finally came to the understanding that Trump believed he could steer the Executive Branch affairs, as well as create national security policies on instinct, depending largely on his personal relationships with international leaders and with a mindset that he was made for television viewership.

I'm not saying that these elements are wrong. In actual sense, all of these elements - instinct and the rest - are a big part of any President's collection. However, there are many more than just those. The workings of presidential decision making come with a truckload of analysis, planning, discipline, evaluating results, and a host of other serious work. This reveals that Trump's transition, along with his first year, was ruined irreversibly. Steps and processes that should've become the norm, particularly for the many Trump advisors, never materialized.

One of my mentors, Paul Laxalt, a former Nevada Senator, loved to say that there are no perfect beginnings as far as politics is concerned. This carefully captures the process of appointments to the topmost Executive Branch positions.

I spent the night of the elections in Fox News studios in Manhattan. I waited all night to air my comment about the foreign-policy priorities of the next President. Everyone expected to see this by 10 pm, after Hilary Clinton had been declared the winner of the elections. I didn't get on the air until about 3 am the next morning. A few observers did believe Trump would win the elections. I find intriguing that just like Robert Dole's failed campaign against Bill Clinton in 1996, Trump's preparations before the polls were rather modest. When compared against Hilary's, it was evident that he was headed for doom. It was, therefore, a rude shock when he won the elections. His campaign team was caught entirely off-guard. Trump had to start over, literally, as his win resulted in fights with the transition volunteers, alongside the scrapping of nearly all its pre-election products. Starting over was a huge call for Trump. Before winning the election, he had very little knowledge about what the Presidential role demanded of him. In the course of the transition, too, he failed to acquire the requisite knowledge, all of which culminated in his poor performance when he assumed office.

CHAPTER 2: CRY "HAVOC!" AND LET SLIP THE DOGS OF WAR

KEY TAKEAWAYS

- On the 7th of April, 2018, Syrian armed forces attacked Douma.
- Trump found Keane's idea of destroying Syria's five main military airfields fascinating.
- Syria was a strategic sideshow.

On the 7th of April, 2018, Syrian armed forces attacked Douma, a city in southwest Syria, alongside other nearby locations. The first set of reports that were released had it that about twelve people were killed, with hundreds of persons wounded. Some of the wounded persons were terribly sick as a result of the dangerous chemicals that were used. Most likely, the base material for the weapons was chlorine. There were, however, indications of sarin gas activity, and possibly some other chemicals. This wasn't the first time something of this nature was happening. A year before, Bashar al-Assad's regime had made use of chemical weapons at Khan Shaykhun in Northwest

Syria. The United States had responded to this attack in just three days, launching fifty-nine missiles at the suspected site.

Apparently, Syria's dictatorship had failed to learn its lesson. Prevention had failed in this case, and the only issue on ground was the way to respond correctly. One year after Khan Shaykhun, the Syrian policy was still in shambles, as it lacked co-ordination on basic objectives and strategy. Worse yet, it was in crisis again. The United States needed to respond to the most recent Syrian chemical weapons attack. At the same time, there was a need for clarity on how to promote American interest in the long run. There was a National Security meeting held a week before the attack on Douma. However, the meeting had pointed in a completely opposite direction, with the United States being advised to withdraw from Syria. If the US did leave, it risked losing the very little gains that the Obama administration was able to achieve and aggravating the threats that Obama's approach fostered. The only person who could do things right was the one who sat at the resolute desk in the oval office.

On the 8th of April, at about 9 am, President Donald Trump tweeted about the attack on Syria in his individual style, and the style familiar to us all today. His tweet contained the fact that many were dead, and that Putin, Russia and Iran Presidents were all responsible for backing Assad up. He actually described Assad as being an animal. Following this tweet, he posted another a few minutes later. This time around, his tweet was directed at Former President Obama, to whom he said that if he crossed his stated Red Line in the Sand, the Syrian disaster would have been brought to an end long ago, and Assad would have been history.

Both statements were clearly forceful. Trump tweeted them without consulting his National Security Team. My predecessor as National Security Advisor, Lieutenant General H. R. McMaster, had left on Friday afternoon. I could not resume my position until Monday. I did try to hold a meeting on Sunday, but the White House lawyers blocked it under the claims that I was not going to be officially recognized as a government employee until Monday. I was frustrated.

On Sunday afternoon, Trump called me. We talked for about twenty minutes- he did most of the talking. Trump pondered on the situation at hand, deliberating that devising a proper means to get out of the Middle East was a tough call. He had repeatedly mentioned this when he called me, occasionally drifting off to matters on trade wars and tariffs. Trump mentioned that he had just seen Jack Keane on Fox News and found Keane's idea of destroying Syria's five main military airfields fascinating. By so doing, Assad's entire air force would be wiped out.

Trump also asked about a National Security Council staffer whom I had it in mind to fire. The staffer was a Trump supporter ever since the earliest days of his presidential campaign. When I mentioned to Trump that the individual was a part of the problem at hand, he was not surprised. Instead, he added that too many people knew too many things. This helped me understand what my most pressing challenge was: Having to deal with the Syria crisis while repositioning the National Security Council's staff to pursue a common goal. At this point, we had to move fast; if not, we would be overtaken by events.

The only thing I could suggest to the National Security Council staff on Sunday was that they do everything within their power to find out everything possible as regards the Assad regime's actions, whether or not there was a likelihood for future attacks to occur. They also needed to develop options for the United States in response. I scheduled a meeting with the National Security Council for 6:45 am on Monday to find out where we stood, as well as examine the roles that Russia and Iran might have played in all of these. Whether we admitted it or not, we needed to make decisions that would fit into a bigger, post-Syria/Iraq picture; decisions that would help us avoid responding in a whack style.

The meeting confirmed my belief, and what seemed to be Trump's belief as well - the strike on Douma required a robust and nothing-short-of-military response. The United States completely opposed the use of weapons of mass destruction. It did not matter whose hands these weapons were in; they endangered the lives of the people of America and our allies.

There was a critical question that kept recurring in the debate. Did reestablishing discouragement against the use of weapons of mass destruction inexorably mean greater US involvement in Syria's civil war? Truth be told, it did not. As a nation, our core interest against chemical-weapons attacks could be justified without ousting Assad, notwithstanding the fears of those who wanted strong action against his regime and those who wanted none. Military force was justified to deter Assad and many others from using chemical, nuclear, or biological weapons in the future. From our perspective, Syria was a strategic sideshow, and whoever ruled there should not distract us from Iran, the real threat.

CHAPTER 3: AMERICA BREAKS FREE

KEY TAKEAWAYS

- When the President introduced me in the light of the Syria strike, I received a standing ovation from the audience.
- The seemingly easy task of preparing Trump for Abe's visit turned out to be a herculean one.
- Trump hated countering America's adversaries through the Sanctions Act because it had Russia as a target.

On the Monday that followed the attack on Syria, I flew to Florida alongside President Trump. It was my first ride on Marine One. We journeyed from the South Lawn to Joint Base Andrews and then flew Air Force One to Miami. We were headed for Hialeah. There, a rally was being hosted to boost Trump's efforts geared towards the creation of a favorable business climate. The rally had well over five hundred persons present, consisting mainly of Cuban and Venezuelan Americans. When the President introduced me in the light of the Syria strike, I received a standing ovation from the audience. Trump was surprised at this move and asked if the people were seriously giving me all the credit. According to him, that signified the end of my job. This was meant to be a joke, or so he thought.

I continued with my job of getting Trump prepared to meet with the Japanese Prime Minister, Abe. I focused much on North-Korea's nuclear weapon program, which was the primary motive for Abe's trip. The seemingly straightforward task of preparing Trump for Abe's visit turned out to be a difficult one. It also revealed things to come. We had made arrangements for two briefings, one of them predominantly on North Korea and security matters, while the other was on trade and economic issues. These briefings were arranged in correspondence to the schedule of meetings between Abe and Trump. The first meeting was on political matters. However, the briefing room was occupied by trade-policy persons who heard that there was a briefing and strolled in. President Trump arrived late, and judging from the people present in the room, I said that we would have a short trade discussion after which we would get back to North Korea. This was my undoing. Trump was riled up by a comment that said we had no better ally than Japan.

He began to complain about Japan's attack on Pearl Harbor. From then on, things took a downturn. Shortly after, Abe arrived, and the session was brought to an end.

Abe and Trump had a meeting one-on-one. Later on, both leaders and their delegations gathered in Mar-a-Lago's White and Gold Ballroom at 3 pm. Abe greeted me by saying, welcome back. Both of us had known each other for more than fifteen years. Like most meetings of this nature, it was only a matter of time before the press mob came in with their cameras rolling. Abe explained to them that in the course of his one-on-one meeting with President Trump, they had both reached a mutual understanding that all options were on the table regarding North Korea, where maximum pressure and the threat of overwhelming military power was needed. When the media left reluctantly, Abe and Trump had a lengthy conversation on North Korea, before turning over to discuss trade issues.

While this meeting was ongoing, the press was busy reporting something else. In the hours before the Syria strike took place, President Trump had agreed initially to impose more sanctions on Russia. Moscow's existence in Syria was vital to sustaining Assad's regime, and maybe, the facilitation of chemical-weapon attacks and a host of other atrocities. However, afterward, President Trump changed his mind. He decided that we had made our point and that we could hit Russia harder if there were ever a need to do so later. In addition, the United States had imposed severe sanctions on Russia on the 6th of April. The imposition of these sanctions was required by the Countering America's Adversaries Through Sanctions Act. Trump hated this act because it had Russia as a target. Trump held a belief that by acknowledging that Russia meddled in US politics, or in that of other European countries, he would indirectly acknowledge that he conspired with Russia during his campaign in 2016. Politically, and logically, this was a very wrong way to have viewed the situation.

CHAPTER 4: THE SINGAPORE SLING

KEY TAKEAWAYS

- In exchange for economic gains, Pyongyang repeatedly sold the idea of negotiation to the United States as well as other countries countless times.
- The South's understanding of our terms to denuclearize North Korea bore no relationship to fundamental US national interests.
- The North declared openly that it was going forward with nuclear and ballistic missile-testing, because it considered itself a nuclear power already.

As we approached a withdrawal from the Iran nuclear deal, Trump began to once again place his focus on North Korea's nuclear-weapons program. I learned a lot, and the more I learned, the greater the discouragement and pessimism I felt towards a Trump-Kim summit. Deep within, I was skeptical of efforts to negotiate the North out of its nuclear weapons program. For crying out loud, Pyongyang had repeatedly sold this very idea of negotiation to the United States as well as other countries countless number of times, in exchange for economic gains. Regardless of the fact that North Korea continually failed to hold up their end of the bargain, they always successfully lured America back onto the negotiating table to make more concessions, yielding time to a proliferator, benefitting indirectly from the delay. We were back at the same spot, again, having failed to learn our lessons. This time, things were even worse. We were validating the commandant of the North Korean prison camp, Kim Jong Un, by allowing him to hold a free meeting with President Trump.

My heart had grown sick and tired from watching Trump's zeal to meet with Kim Jong Un. I had endured eight years of Obama's mistakes. Somewhere at the back of my mind, I always feared that Obama would make the mistake of conceding dangerously to North Korea as his Iran policy did. There was also the Bush 43 Administration's failed Six-Party Talks and Clinton's failed Agreed Framework.

On the 12th of April, I met the Director of the National Security Office of South Korea, Chung Eui-Yong.

Sometime in March, back in the Oval Office, Chung had informed Trump of Kim's invitation to meet with him. Trump accepted the invitation immediately. Chung would later admit that from the very beginning, it was he who suggested to Kim that he make the invitation. The entire thing was a creation of South Korea. It was more related to their unification agenda than genuine strategy on Kim's part, or ours.

From my point of view, the South's understanding of our terms to denuclearize North Korea bore no relationship to fundamental US national interests. I considered it devoid of substance, and nothing else but a risky theatrical display. I admonished Chung not to discuss the denuclearization at the North-South summit scheduled to hold on the 27th of April in a bid to prevent Pyongyang from driving a wedge between South Korea, Japan, and the United States. I made it clear to Trump that we were in need of the closest relationship we could foster with Moon-Jae to avoid North Korea's engineering a split between Washington and Seoul. I was bent on preserving the US-South Korean alignment and avoiding a scandalous headline for the President. Trump wasn't bothered.

Later that morning, I got to meet with my counterpart from Japan- Shotaro Yachi. As soon as possible, Yachi wanted me to hear their perspective. Tokyo viewed the Trump-Kim meeting as 180 degrees from South Korea's, almost the same picture as mine. According to Yachi, they firmly held that the North was highly determined to get nuclear weapons and that we were inching close to the last chance to arrive at a peaceful solution. Japan was unwilling to have anything to do with the action for action formula that characterized Bush 43's failed Six-Party Talks. On the surface, action for action appeared to make good sense, but it worked solely to benefit North Korea. Kim Jong Un completely understood this, just as well as we did.

On the 21st of April, the North declared openly that it was going forward with nuclear and ballistic missile-testing, because it considered itself a nuclear power already. The media saw this as a significant step forward, and even President Trump himself called it big progress. All I saw was another propaganda looming. If all the testing were concluded, Pyongyang could quickly finish up all the work that had to do with weapons and delivery-system production capability. Chung returned on the 24th of April, just before Moon's inter-Korean summit with Kim. I had some sense of relief knowing that Chung intended that the leaders' Panmunjom Declaration would only be two pages long. This simply meant that whatever it said, or had to do with denuclearization could not be pretty specific. I also had a feeling that South Korea believed Kim Jong Un was desperate for a deal because of the pressure mounted by sanctions, and that the North's top priority was economic development since it was a nuclear-weapons state. Personally, I found this reasoning discomforting. All the while, Pompeo was getting things set, timing, and location wise for the meeting between Trump and Kim.

CHAPTER 5: A TALE OF THREE CITIES - SUMMITS IN BRUSSELS, LONDON, AND HELSINKI

KEY TAKEAWAYS

- Three summits held in July, back-to-back.
- Trump really wanted Putin to visit Washington.
- Putin blamed the decline in America-Russia relations on the domestic politics of the United States.

Following June's Singapore encounter with Kim Jong Un, three summits were held in July, back-to-back. The three summits were a NATO meeting in Brussels that had been scheduled long ago, Trump and Theresa May's meeting in London and Trump and Putin in Helsinki. Before Trump left Washington, he said that he had NATO, the UK, and Putin and that in all honesty, Putin might be the easiest of all three. I realized in the course of that busy July that President Trump did not follow any international strategy, nor did he even have a consistent trajectory. He basically thought in bits and left the rest of us to connect the pieces. This had both good sides and bad.

After the Singapore meeting, I traveled around various European capitals preparing for the different summits that were to hold. One of the trips I planned was to Moscow. It came with complications of its own. I told Trump that I was going to Moscow to lay the foundation and get the groundwork for his trip started, and he asked if I had to travel to Russia. He also asked if I couldn't do whatever it was over a telephone call. He did not object when I explained why and how our preparations would benefit from me reviewing the issues in advance. Afterward, I asked Kelly why Trump complained, and Kelly said Trump was worried that I was going to upstage him. Let's think about it. Besides Trump, a statement like this would sound ridiculous for any President. It might have seemed flattering, but if it were true, it signaled some sort of danger. I wondered what to do to overcome the problem, but I failed to come up with a good answer.

If there was anything Trump really wanted, it was for Putin to visit Washington. However, the Russians had no intention of doing such. At the time, we had been going back and forth over possible meeting venues, with Helsinki and Vienna being our major options. Russia pushed for Vienna while we wanted Helsinki. At the end of the day, it turned out that Trump wasn't even keen on Helsinki. He kept insisting that Finland was a part of Russia. I attempted explaining the history to him, but before I got anywhere, he said he also wanted Vienna. He then told me to tell the Russians that we'll do whatever they want. However, we were finally able to agree on Helsinki after some more jockeying, of course.

On the 26th of June, I arrived at Moscow's Vnukovo airport. The next morning, I went to the Spaso house, where the longtime US Ambassador in Moscow was resident. Jon Huntsman had put together a breakfast with Russian influencers and think-tankers. Inclusive of these persons was the former Foreign Minister, Igor Ivanov. I had known and worked with him in the course of the Bush 43 Administration. There were also members of the National Security Council and embassy officials present. Unanimously, the Russians believed that the American views about Russia had not changed, regardless of whether they were the congress's views or those held by the general public.

This was true. I placed a lot of weight on the issue of election-interference, knowing fully well that most of those present would quickly report to their contacts in the Kremlin and more broadly. I wanted the word out.

Our delegation, alongside Huntsman, went off to the Russian Federation Security Council's offices to meet with our counterparts. The offices were located on Staraya Ploshad. The Secretary of the Russian Council, Nikolai Patrushev, was not in the country at the time. We, however, had a complete team on either side to cover all the issues on ground. At some point in time, Putin himself was the Secretary of the Russian Security Council, briefly though. Patrushev had succeeded him as FSB Director. Patrushev was still very close to Putin.

We had lunch with Russian Foreign Minister Sergei Lavrov at the Osobnyak guesthouse, an estate owned in pre-revolutionary times by a wealthy industrialist who sympathized with the Bolsheviks, and where I had been a frequent guest. Once again, I laid emphasis on the election interference issue, and Lavrov dodged it by remarking that hackers could not be ruled out and that the Russian government had nothing to do with it.

We rode to the Kremlin to meet with Putin at about 2:30 pm. We arrived there early, and while we waited, the defense minister, Sergei Shoygu, who was present with a military delegation, came over and introduced himself. He also joined the Putin meeting later on. We were ushered into a room where the main event was slated, which I remembered most certainly as the very room where I met Putin in 2001. Pressmen and women were already there. I was instructed by the Russian protocol officers to wait in the center of the room for Putin to greet me. We both shook hands for the camera. Putin seemed very relaxed and self-assured. I also went on to greet Lavrov, Shoygu, and Putin's diplomatic ambassador, Yuri Ushakov. Afterward, we all sat down at the beautiful conference table.

With the media present, Putin began by noting that there was a decline in relations between America and Russia. He blamed it all on the domestic politics of the United States. I refused to take the bait, knowing fully well that he had the home court, and this kind of competition would not be to my advantage. Since Moscow was then hosting the 2018 FIFA World Cup, and the US (with Mexico and Canada) had just won the games for 2026, I replied that I looked forward to hearing from him how to stage a successful World Cup. The press then cleared out in a disciplined way, and we got down to business.

CHAPTER 6: THWARTING RUSSIA

KEY TAKEAWAYS

- I had looked forward to extricating the United States from the Intermediate-Range Nuclear Forces, popularly called the INF Treaty.
- For years, Russia had been violating the INF Treaty.
- The INF Treaty bound only two nations of the world, with one of them cheating.

Ever since my days in George Bush's Administration, I had looked forward to extricating the United States from the Intermediate-Range Nuclear Forces, popularly called the INF Treaty. I know this might sound like an impossible task, but I had been there before. I knew exactly what to do. I helped Bush get America out of the 1972 ABM Treaty, which I describe as both dangerous and outmoded. This decision prohibited the United States from launching an effective national missile defense. There really wasn't any learning curve. One of Helsinki's outcomes was increased cooperation between the US and the Russian national security councils; the tools were at hand. I proposed to Nikolai Patrushev we meet in Geneva, and he agreed that we meet on the 23rd of August.

For years, Russia had been violating the INF Treaty. All these years, America stayed in compliance and watched Russia do their thing. In order to prevent a nuclear war from breaking out in Europe, the Reagan-Gorbachev agreement between the US and the USSR barred missiles and launchers ranging between 500 and 5,500 kilometers. Over time, however, the purpose for which the INF was created became severely violated by Russian breaches that seemed unending, global strategic realities that changed, and even technological progress. Before President Trump assumed office, Russia had begun the deployment of missiles. This violated the INF's prohibitions in the Kaliningrad exclave on the Baltic Sea, which laid the basis for a substantial threat to NATO's European members. Also, the treaty bound no other countries.

The honest-to-God truth was that the INF Treaty bound only two nations of the world, with one of the cheating. As things stood, only one country in the world was prohibited from developing intermediate-range missiles: The United States. Even if this made sense then, it makes no sense at all today.

Patrushev and I got to meet at the US Mission to the United Nations. This took place in Geneva. Prior to this time, the staff of the NSC had held extensive consultations with the United States government on the agenda. Pompeo and I had discussed arms-control issues numerous times, and he agreed with my approach to Patrushev. Adopting the classic Cold War-style, Patrushev and I began with arms control and non-proliferation, especially Iran and North Korea. The Russians focused on strategic ability, following after Putin's approach in our Moscow meeting. This strategic ability discourse was their primary phrase for attacking us for having withdrawn from the ABM Treaty. Their assertions had it that missile defense was inherently destabilizing strategically, and they clearly wanted more-detailed negotiations between the two security councils on this proposition. Quickly, I disabused them of that notion. I explained to them, again, that we withdrew from the ABM Treaty for the purpose of dealing with threats to the homeland from emerging nuclear-weapons states and accidental launches from Russia and China.

Patrushev remarked, saying our levels of trust respectively, would define how successful we will be. He pointed to the INF Treaty, claiming that the claims of compliance were conflicting. Pure propaganda, if you ask me. For more than ten years, Russia had consistently violated the INF Treaty. In the course of Obama's Administration, the point was raised repeatedly, but nothing was one about it. Like all other US Treaties, the Defense and State Departments had way too many lawyers, that even if we ever wanted to violate a Treaty, we couldn't.

Like always, the Russians came up with a long list of alleged US violations that they planned on discussing in detail. The ironic thing was that we had a longer list of actual Russian violations that I didn't intend to waste time on. We considered the possibility of universalizing the INF by bringing other countries in. Still, it was a mere dream to think that Iran, China, and others would willingly destroy tons of their existing missile arsenals to comply with the treaty's terms. Instead of fantasizing about that, I wanted to make clear the fact that the US could withdraw from the INF, even though the US held no official position.

I also mentioned that it was not likely for us to agree to a five-year extension of Obama's New START, one which Moscow and most US liberals were praying for. We had several reasons against succumbing to a knee-jerk extension, one of which included the need to involve China in strategic weapons negotiations for the first time. I could tell that this view surprised the Russians. We also needed to cover tactical nuclear weapons and the new and improved technologies that Russia and China were in the aggressive pursuit of. Lastly, we had to consider a return to the conceptually far simpler model of the 2002 Treaty of Moscow, which I also negotiated by the way.

When I returned to Washington, I spent the next couple of months preparing for our withdrawal from the INF. To prevent leaks that were capable of agitating the press and foreign-policy establishment, I believed we should follow a quiet, low-profile, but accelerated approach, instead of holding endless meetings among staffers who had lived with the INF Treaty their entire government careers and couldn't bear to see it die. I believed Trump was on board, although I was never certain if he understood that the INF Treaty did not regulate nuclear weapons as such. I wanted to launch

US withdrawal from the treaty, or even mutual withdrawal, before my next meeting with Patrushev. Experience had taught me that without action-forcing deadlines, governments could fight change with incredible persistence and success.

CHAPTER 7: TRUMP HEADS FOR THE DOOR IN SYRIA AND AFGHANISTAN, AND CAN'T FIND IT.

KEY TAKEAWAYS

- The war by radical Islamist terrorists against the United States will continue much longer than this.
- Syria emerged once more through Turkey's incarceration of Pastor Andrew Brunson.

Long before 9/11, the war by radical Islamist terrorists against the United States had begun. These wars will continue much longer than this. I'm fully aware that you may not like the sound of that, but beyond what you want or not, this is the reality of things.

Donald Trump did not like it. More so, he acted like it was untrue. Over and over again, Trump opposed perpetual wars in the Middle East without a concrete plan for what followed after withdrawing US forces and effectively abandoning critical regional allies as the withdrawal unfolded. Wrongly, Trump would say that it was all thousands of miles away. Unlike Trump, however, during my tenure at the White House, I tried to operate realistically. Sometimes, I was successful. At other times, I wasn't.

Following our retaliation in April for Assad's chemical-weapons attack on Douma, Syria emerged once more, but this time, indirectly. The reemergence was done through Turkey's incarceration of Pastor Andrew Brunson. Brunson was an apolitical evangelical preacher who, along with his family, had lived and worked in Turkey for twenty years, before he was arrested in 2016. His arrest came after a failed military coup against President Recep Tayyip Erdogan. There was more. Brunson was also charged for conspiring with followers of Fethullah Gulen, an Islamic teacher living in America, once an Erdogan ally, but now an enemy obsessively denounced as a terrorist.

When Trump returned from Helsinki, Erdogan placed a call across to follow up on the short encounter they had at NATO. He also called to inquire about Brunson and his relationship with Gulen. In addition, Erdogan asked about Mehmet Atilla's conviction. Mehmet Atilla was a senior official of the Turkish bank- Halkbank, who was convicted for financial fraud, which stemmed from massive violations of Iranian sanctions. This particular ongoing investigation was a threat to Erdogan himself because of several allegations that claimed he and his family used Halkbank for their personal purposes. These purposes were also alleged to be facilitated further when his son-in-law became the Finance Minister in Turkey. As far as Erdogan was concerned, Gulen and his movement were to be held responsible for the Halkbank charges, so it was all part of a conspiracy against him, not to mention against his family's growing wealth. He wanted the Halkbank case dropped, something that seemed very unlikely, mainly because US prosecutors had their eyes all over the bank and its fraudulent operations. Besides these, Turkey might end up getting mandatory sanctions for the reason that pending legislation in Congress would halt the sale of F-35s to Turkey because Ankara was purchasing Russia's S-400 air defense system. There was a whole lot for Erdogan to worry about.

Trump, however, did not appear to want so much. He only wanted to know when Brunson would be released to return to America, to which he thought Erdogan had given his word. Erdogan said only that the Turkish judicial process was continuing, and Brunson was no longer imprisoned, but under house arrest in Izmir, Turkey. Trump told Erdogan that he did not find that very helpful because all he needed to hear was that Brunson was coming home. He went on to stress his friendship with Erdogan, but in the light of things, it was clear that it would be difficult for him to fix the hard issues facing the US-Turkey relationship unless Brunson returned to the US.

CHAPTER 8: CHAOS AS A WAY OF LIFE

KEY TAKEAWAYS

- Numerous incongruent issues and individuals joined to push the Administration even deeper into unknown terrain.
- Trump generally had only two intelligence briefings per week.
- Trump was annoyingly vindictive, and he constantly demonstrated this by erupting against John McCain, even after McCain died and could do him no more harm.

After I arrived at the White House, it took me about a month to have a chance to assess the way things worked inside. In many ways, dysfunctionality arose. More often than not, these dysfunctionalities unfolded through specific policy issues.

There was more. Towards the end of 2018, and the early months of 2019, about eight to nine months after I arrived at the White House, numerous seemingly incongruent issues and individuals joined in pushing the Administration even deeper into unknown terrains.

For example, in June 2018, Kelly tried a tactic on Trump's schedule. He began each day in the Oval with what he called Chief-of-Staff time at 11 am. He did this in the hopes that he would minimize the rambling lectures he delivered during his twice-weekly intelligence briefings. One thing was striking. People had come to find out that officially, Trump's day did not begin until when it was almost lunchtime. It wasn't that Trump was loafing around in the mornings. No. He actually spent a great deal of time working the phones in the residence. Trump made calls to all manners of people, which included US government officials. He also spoke at length with people outside of the government. To contemporary Presidents, this was an anomaly.

Trump's day was a huge contrast from what a regular day was for President George H.W. Bush. Bush's first Chief of Staff, former Governor John Sununu, described Bush's day as beginning in the Oval Office with an intelligence briefing at 8:00 am. This briefing was said to have the President, the vice president, the National Security Advisor, and Chief of Staff in attendance. There was a lot that this meeting covered that it ended only at 9:15 am.

If I were opportune to have such an orderly day, I would have thought I had died and gone to heaven. Trump generally had only two intelligence briefings per week, and in most of those, he spoke at greater length than the briefers. Most times, he spoke on matters that were in no way related to the subjects at hand.

Trump also had an extremely annoying schedule. He was annoyingly vindictive, and he constantly demonstrated this by erupting against John McCain, even after McCain died and could do Trump no more harm. On the 15th of August as well, Trump decided to revoke former CIA Director, John Brennan's security clearance. Brennan was no prize, and in the course of his tenure, the CIA became more involved in politics than at any other time in its history. Brannan denied any improper behavior. However, Trump was convinced Brennan was extremely caught up in abusing the FISA surveillance process to spy on his 2016 campaign, all of which was aggravated by his constant presence in the media disapproving Trump after he assumed office.

The media fixed firmly on the revocation immediately after Sanders publicized it during her daily briefing at noon. Kelly informed me that the Brennan case was exploding. We both had a long conversation where we went over what had happened. Kelly said that by mid to late July, he thought he had gotten Trump off the idea of taking away people's clearances, but Trump returned to it because his favorite media sources kept pounding away on it.

Earlier that day, Trump wanted to revoke clearances from a longer list of names. However, he settled for Sanders reading the names out at the briefing, indirectly threatening to revoke the clearances sometime in the future. I thought there was a case against Brennan for politicizing the CIA, but Trump had obscured it by the blatantly political approach he took. It would only get worse if more clearances were lifted. Kelly agreed with me on this.

CHAPTER 9: VENEZUELA LIBRE

KEY TAKEAWAYS

- Venezuela presented the Trump-led government with an opportunity.
- Several press stories repeated specifics of what we had repeatedly heard from the Opposition in 2019.
- Maduro's regime was autocratic.

Venezuela, in the course of its unlawful, tyrannical regime, presented the Trump-led government with an opportunity. The opportunity required a steady amount of determination and constant pressure on our part. We failed to meet this standard. Trump was upset, as he continually wavered and bobbed, aggravating internal Administration disagreements rather than resolving them, and continuously obstructing our efforts to carry out a policy. Right from time, we were never quite sure of success with supporting the Venezuelan Opposition's efforts to replace Nicolas Maduro, Hugo Chavez's heir. As a matter of fact, we felt the opposite. Maduro's Opposition took a step in January 2019 because they thought that this could be their last shot at freedom after several years of trying and failing repeatedly. The only reason America responded to this call was that it was a matter of national interest. Up until now, it still is.

Following the failure of our efforts to oust Maduro, the Trump Administration was in no way hesitant to discuss publicly, in detail, how close the Opposition had come to ousting Maduro, and what had gone wrong. Several press stories repeated specifics of what we had repeatedly heard from the Opposition in 2019. This was barely a regular situation of diplomatic discussions and exchanges. We heard from members of Congress, private US citizens, particularly members of the Cuban-American and Venezuelan-American communities in Florida. In the future, when Venezuela is unrestricted again, the many individuals supportive of the Opposition will be free to tell their stories openly. Until then, we only have the memories of people like myself fortunate enough to tell their stories for them.

In Venezuela, there is a twenty-year-long history of missed opportunities, considering the firmly held Opposition to the Chavez-Maduro regime. A short while after I became the National security advisor, Maduro was speaking at a military awards ceremony on the 4th of August, where two drones attacked him. Although the attack failed, it showed greatly that there was dissent within the military. There were also the ridiculous pictures of a service member who fled at the sound of the explosions, showing how disloyal the army was to Maduro.

Maduro's regime was autocratic. Not only was it autocratic, but it was also a threat due to its Cuba connection and the openings it afforded Russia, China, and Iran. Moscow's threat was undisputable, military and financial wise, having spent significant funds to buttress Maduro, control Venezuela's oil-and-gas business, and enforce costs on the U.S.

Venezuela was a threat on its own. This fact was demonstrated in an incident that took place at sea, along the Guyana-Venezuela border on the 22nd of August. Venezuelan naval units tried to board ExxonMobil exploration ships, under licenses from Guyana in its territorial waters. Chavez and Maduro had run Venezuela's oil-and-gas industry into a ditch, and extensive hydrocarbon resources in Guyana would pose an immediate competitive threat right next door. The incident evaporated as the exploration ships, after refusing Venezuelan requests to land a chopper on board one of them, headed rapidly back into Guyanese waters.

CHAPTER 10: THUNDER OUT OF CHINA

KEY TAKEAWAYS

- As far back as 1978, Deng Xiaoping made a decision to shift Chinese economic policy away from the prevailing Marxism.
- The United States also made a decision to recognize the People's republic of China in 1979.
- After joining the World Trade Organization, China did the exact opposite of what was predicted.

In the twenty-first century, the economic and geopolitical relationship between China and America would shape the state of international affairs. As far back as 1978, Deng Xiaoping decided to shift Chinese economic policy away from the regular Marxism. The United States also made a decision to recognize the People's republic of China in 1979, thereby derecognizing the Republic of China on Taiwan. Both were crucial points. How these decisions came to be, and the after-effects they had are rather complicated, but the strategy adopted by the US, and the West's broad and more informed public opinion for decades afterward, rested on two main propositions.

The first was that those who were in support of these developments believed that China would be changed irreversibly by the rising prosperity caused by market-oriented policies, more significant foreign investment, ever-deeper interconnections with global markets, and broader acceptance of international economic norms. According to the phrase, China was bound to enjoy a peaceful rise and become a responsible stakeholder in international affairs. The apotheosis of this assessment was bringing China into the World Trade Organization. This happened in 2001.

The second was that those in support of the benevolent view of China's rise held that it was almost inevitable that as China's wealth increased as a nation, democracy would. The patterns of free elections, which had been seen in local, isolated villages in China, would spread to other locales and provinces and finally rise to the national level. They mentioned that there was a strong correlation between the growth of economic freedom and the rise of true middle classes, on the one hand, and political freedom and democracy on the other. They further argued that as China became more democratic, the democratic peace theory's repercussions would take effect. These consequences included the fact that firstly, China would begin to avoid competition for regional or global dominion. Secondly, the world would avoid the Thucydides trap. Lastly, the risk of international conflict, hot or cold, would regress.

However, both of these views were very incorrect, fundamentally. After joining the World Trade Organization, China did the exact opposite of what was predicted. China did not adhere to the existing norms. In fact, China played the organization, and successfully pursued a mercantilist policy in a purportedly free-trade body. As though that wasn't enough, China went on to steal intellectual properties, forced technology transfers from, and discriminated against business investors and businesses engaged in corrupt practices with all of these done on an international scale. Worst of all, China continued to manage its domestic economy in statist, brutal ways. The primary targets of all China's structural aspects were countries like America, Europe, Japan, and virtually all industrial democracies, plus others that are neither but were still victims. In addition, China sought political and military benefits from economic activities that free-market societies do not consider. China was able to achieve this by allegedly privately-owned companies, which in truth were tools of China's military and intelligence services through the fusion of its civil and military power centers, and by engaging in aggressive cyber warfare that targeted foreign private interests as much or more than government secrets.

On the political scene, China began to move away from being democratic, rather than moving towards it. As of now, Xi Jinping in China has the most powerful leader as well as the most centralized control of the government since Mao Tse-tung.

CHAPTER 11: CHECKING INTO THE HANOI HILTON, THEN CHECKING OUT, AND THE PANMUNJOM PLAYTIME

KEY TAKEAWAYS

- Trump was highly fascinated with the idea of securing a deal with the North.
- Trump said that he could not lift sanctions until North Korea denuclearized, or he would appear like a fool.
- There was a possibility that Pompeo was not fully aware that Biegun was so resolute on his personal agenda to get a deal.

Following the conclusion of the 2018 congressional elections, the chances of escaping another Trump-Kim summit was very slim. Trump was highly fascinated with the idea of obtaining a deal with the North. This fascination waxed and waned, but with six months having passed since the Singapore summit held, and nothing much happening, waxing was becoming dominant. Pompeo was supposed to meet with Kim Yong Chol of North Korea in New York on the 8th of

November. The same day, or the day after, Kim wanted another White House meeting to hold. Luckily for me, I would be in Paris preparing for Trump's upcoming visit, to ensure that the spring 2018 scene would not be repeated. I still cringed at the thought of Kim Yong Chol back in the Oval. Fortunately, Kim Jong Un canceled the trip. At that point, the prospects of having a Moon-Kim submit too didn't seem to be headed anywhere. At the very best, it would be kicked into 2019.

After New Year's, however, the pace increased. It didn't take so much to get Trump fired up. Kim Jong Un unexpectedly flew to Beijing on his birthday, the 8th of January, likely to prepare for another Trump meeting. As expected, there was a visit to Washington by Kin Yong Chol on the 17th and 18th of January, with a Trump meeting on the 18th. I couldn't wait for it. I had to explain to Pompeo that I had a minor surgery that had been long scheduled for that day. Along with him, Kim Yong Chol brought another letter from Kim Jong Un. The oval office meeting lasted ninety minutes, and truth be told, I preferred to have surgery. Charlie Kupperman also attended the session. He reported that the discussion rambled, typically, and that the use of loose language was uncontrolled. Nonetheless, he mentioned that he saw no real commitment from Trump and that in the end, Trump said that he could not lift sanctions until North Korea denuclearized, or he would appear like a fool. This was true, and it was good to know that Trump still remembered it. In many cases, that may not be the grand strategy. However, at a time like that, it was what we had to work with.

Over the weekend, in Sweden, staff-level negotiations were scheduled. This was when I began to fear that things would start to slip out of control. Shortly after, according to press reports, it seemed very likely, especially since North Korea had finally named a counterpart to the State Department's special envoy Steve Biegun- Kim Hyok Chol, a veteran of the Bush 43–era Six-Party Talks. This was in no way a good sign.

The summit venue and dates for Hanoi had been fixed for the 27th and 28th of February. I genuinely thought about how to prevent a debacle. At Stanford, Biegun had made remarks that suggested that the Administration was ready to follow the action for action formula demanded by North Korea. This heightened my concern, worsened by the State Department's reversion to type: unhelpful and silent on what they were telling the North Koreans. The State Department had done the very same thing to the National Security Council during the Six-Party Talks. There was a possibility that Pompeo was not fully aware that Biegun was so resolute on his personal agenda to get a deal. However, whether or not Pompeo was responsible for ordering, allowing, or even being ignorant of Biegun's enthusiasm wasn't the issue. The consequences were dangerous, and this was the real deal.

CHAPTER 12: TRUMP LOSES HIS WAY, AND THEN HIS NERVE

KEY TAKEAWAYS

- If at any point, US attention to Iran faded, for Trump especially, I knew very well that Tehran would help us return it to the top of his agenda.
- Death to America meant death to Trump, John Bolton and Pompeo.
- The biggest form of opposition came from the government's permanent bureaucracy.
- It concluded that a government entity like the revolutionary guard was capable of receiving the designation.

If US attention to Iran faded at any point in time, for Trump especially, I knew very well that Tehran would help us return it to the top of his agenda. Hence, it was a big issue when Iran's supreme leader, the Ayatollah Khamenei, offered a constructive explanation of what Iran's protesters intended when they chanted Death to America, alongside Death to Israel. Death to America, he explained, meant death to Trump, John Bolton, and

Pompeo. These eruptions of truth, like who Iran's leaders were targeting for death, reminded us of the constant need to exert pressure on Tehran. This wasn't due only to Iran's nuclear-weapons and ballistic-missile programs, but also to its continual role as the world's primary hub for terrorism, as well as its strong military presence across the Middle East.

One particular issue of contention was whether or not to designate the Islamic Revolutionary Guard Corps as a Foreign Terrorist Organization, which was a legal term that carried specified consequences for the organization named such. Me, Pompeo and Trump wanted this designation because having to deal with a group so listed, and its agents risked charges of felony. Mnuchin was worried that this designation for the elite wing of the Iranian military or even for the Quds Force, its expeditionary arm deployed abroad, currently, in Iraq, Syria, Lebanon, and Yemen would have widespread consequences, a concern I didn't understand. I thought that the point of the whole thing was to ensure that these terrorists were inflicted with as much pain as possible. Other agencies held different positions, but the crux of it all was being able to leave well enough alone without making more work for us.

The most prominent form of opposition came from the government's permanent bureaucracy. The attorneys in the State Department's Legal Advisor's Office held the issue for months, without informing the Legal Advisor herself. The attorneys at Homeland Security also did the same thing, as they all hoped the problem would just go away. During our efforts in March 2019 to move the process along, most of the lawyer time in many key agencies were consumed by disputes over how to fund Trump's Mexico border wall, which had long been the Administration's very own La Brea tar pit. There were several legal issues, including whether the related statute allowed designation all or part of a government as a Foreign Terrorist Organization or whether the law only applied to non-state actors; Al-Qaeda, for instance. This matter was split in March 2019 by the Justice Department's Office of Legal Counsel. It concluded that a government entity like the revolutionary guard was capable of receiving the designation. However, it frowned against the designation being received by an entire government. This conclusion, which I describe as being Solomonic, restricted the possible impact of the decision. I did not see this as an addition in any way, but we were only after the guard. Thus, it seemed unproductive to engage in further conceptual debate.

CHAPTER 13: FROM THE AFGHANISTAN COUNTERTERRORISM MISSION TO THE CAMP DAVID NEAR MISS

KEY TAKEAWAYS

- A poor presentation or bad timing of these objectives would result in another outburst.
- Pompeo believed that Khalilzad was carrying out Trump's mandate to negotiate a deal, lowering the US troop presence to zero.
- I had to make the Defense Department's presentation to Trump scheduled to hold the next Friday as effective as possible.

I knew what I wanted to achieve in Afghanistan. Luckily for me, Trump's other senior advisors reasoned along with me and shared the same objectives as I did. There were two of those objectives. The first was to prevent the potential resurgence of ISIS and al-Qaeda and their attendant threats of terrorist attacks against America. The second was to remain vigilant against the nuclear-weapons programs in Iran on the west and Pakistan on the east. This was the anti-terrorism platform we intended to pursue in the early part of 2019. There was the hard part to this, though, and it was basically getting Trump first to agree, and secondly, to stick with his decision. A poor presentation or lousy timing of these objectives would result in another outburst in which Trump would demand we withdraw everyone immediately; not presenting them meant withdrawal by default.

Another layer of complexity was found in Zalmay Khalilzad's ongoing negotiations with the Taliban. Pompeo strongly believed that Khalilzad was carrying out Trump's mandate to negotiate a deal lowering the US troop presence to zero. Personally, I thought that this was clearly a bad policy. The United States government, in theory, opposed any arrangement of such except it was based on certain conditions. This meant that we would go to zero only if the country were free of terrorism activities, ISIS and Al-Qaeda were restricted totally from establishing operating bases, and we had sufficient, adequate means of verification. I saw this as being naïve. How on earth did we expect to make a deal with miscreants and they would adhere to it?

From the very beginning, Pompeo claimed that it was the Pentagon that sought a deal with the Taliban, to reduce threats to US personnel as we reduced our presence. He also claimed that in the absence of such an agreement, the risks to the shrinking US forces were too high. Again, I felt this was a somewhat childlike approach. I never understood why such a deal gave us any real protection from a group of terrorists we had never trusted.

In the Afghan context, conditions based was like an opiate. It made some persons feel good. However, it was a momentary, eventually muffled experience at best. I disbelieved that there was any deal with the Taliban we should find acceptable, given their track record. If total withdrawal were the goal, desecrations of the conditions would not change that outcome, given Trump's view. Once we were on the nosedive to zero, that's where we would finish. But if continuing negotiations bought us time to prepare and maintain a sustainable anti-terrorism presence, then it was worth the play.

Myself, Shanahan, Dunford, and Pompeo believed that the earlier we briefed Trump on how such processes would work in practice, the better. A briefing was scheduled for Friday, 15th of March, and preparations for it began. We knew how much was at stake, so we had a prep session in the Tank on the Friday before. Out of curiosity, Pompeo made John Sullivan attend in his stead. Maybe he didn't want to reveal what the actual state of play in diplomacy with the Taliban was before the Trump briefing, which would be constant with his practice of sharing as little about the negotiations as he could. I wasn't particularly bothered by his absence. I had concluded that Afghan diplomacy wouldn't matter much in the long run anyway.

I had a more limited horizon: to make the Defense Department's presentation to Trump scheduled to hold the next Friday as effective as possible, thereby persuading him that we needed to keep considerable anti-terrorism resources in the country.

CHAPTER 14: THE END OF THE IDYLL

KEY TAKEAWAYS

- Ukraine appears an improbable place as a battleground to risk an American presidency.
- Ukraine is under serious Russian political and economic burden.
- Russia did not withdraw or alter its aggressive behavior in any significant way during the Obama Administration.
- Through the rest of my White House tenure, Volker was a regular visitor, who kept me in the loop on his efforts.

Ukraine appears an unlikely place as a battleground to risk an American presidency. However, that is precisely what occurred in 2019, literally just days following my resignation. I couldn't have timed it better. I participated in and witnessed much of the disaster as it unfolded. I also appeared poised, for good or ill, to figure in only the fourth serious effort to impeach a President in American history. In all of my West Wing tenure, Trump always wanted to do that which he wanted to do, based on his knowledge and personal interests. In Ukraine, it appeared as though he was finally able to have it all.

Ukraine is under severe Russian political and economic burdens. In 2014, Moscow arranged the unlawful invasion of Crimea after overruling militarily, the first change in European borders due to military force since 1945. Russian troops remained positioned across the Donbas region in eastern Ukraine, supporting and guiding nationalist forces there. This major Russian-American clash shows that the failure to act earlier to bring Ukraine into NATO left this vast, critically important country susceptible to Putin's effort to rebuild Russian hegemony in the former Soviet Union space.

At NATO's April 2008 Bucharest Summit, the Bush 43 Administration tried to put Georgia and Ukraine on a path to NATO membership, which the Europeans, especially Germany and France, opposed. The catastrophic penalties were made bare that August, when Russian troops attacked Georgia, successfully placing two provinces under Moscow's control. This has remained so up until today.

Ukraine's suffering began later, but the pattern remained the same. Following this was Western sanctions. Russia did not withdraw nor alter its aggressive behavior in any significant way during the Obama Administration, recognizing the intense weakness Obama projected on a global scale.

Trump inherited this tragedy. He, however, paid very little attention to it in his first two years in office. In 2017, Tillerson appointed Kurt Volker as Special Representative for Ukraine Negotiations. I met Volker for the first time in this capacity on May 10, 2018, when he defined his role and priorities. Then, he advocated a non-recognition policy on Russia's annexation of Crimea, as well as its military presence in the Donbas. Through the rest of my White House tenure, Volker was a regular visitor, who kept me in the loop on his efforts. I found him professional and helpful as I engaged with my European counterparts on Ukraine and related issues.

The first major encounter I had with Ukraine itself in the Trump Administration was in 2018. I flew to Kyiv to celebrate the August 24 anniversary of Ukraine's 1991 declaration of independence from the Soviet Union. In

2017, Jim Mattis had attended this ceremony. Like me, he felt the need to demonstrate the US' resolve in support of Ukraine's sustained independence and practicability. Besides, considering Russia's one-sided annexation of Crimea and the apparent Russian assistance to and control over opposition forces in eastern Ukraine, this worry was definitely not imaginary.

CHAPTER 15: EPILOGUE

KEY TAKEAWAYS

- I do not know who the whistleblower is.
- I did know more than I wanted to about Trump's management of Ukraine affairs.

On the 10th of September 2019, when I resigned as National Security Advisor, no one predicted the saga that followed: The Trump impeachment saga. Then, I wasn't aware of the famous whistleblower's complaint, nor its handling in the Executive Branch. However, both the complaint and the publicity it received afterward changed the Washington political landscape in completely unforeseen ways.

I do not know who the whistleblower is.

Anyway, I did know more than I wanted to about Trump's management of Ukraine affairs. While the entire nation focused on the unfolding events as it concerned impeachment, I focused on determining what my private and legal responsibilities were pertaining to that information. Whether Trump's conduct rose to the level of an impeachable offense, I had found it extremely troubling. That was why I informed the White House Counsel, Pat Cipollone, his staff, and Attorney General Bill Barr. I also informed them about why Pompeo, Mnuchin, and I had worried over it in our own conversations. The importance of preserving the President's constitutional authority and what Hamilton was no small matter either.

In the following partisan Armageddon, virtue signalers on both sides of the battle were quick to tell the world how easy the choices were. I didn't see it that way.